soho theatre + writers' centre

Soho Theatre Company and Wax Lips Theatre Company present

NAVY PIER

by **John Corwin**

First performed in the UK at Soho Theatre and Writers' Centre, 21 Dean St, W1 on 11 September 2000.

Soho Theatre Company is supported by stone
Performances in the Lorenz Auditorium. Regd. Charity No: 267234

soho
theatre + writers' centre

NAVY PIER
by **John Corwin**

Martin Joseph May
Liv Doraly Rosen
Iris Paloma Baeza
Kurt Oliver Milburn

Director Abigail Morris
Designer Jonathan Fensom
Lighting Designer Jason Taylor

Assistant Director Tessa Walker
Second Assistant Elizabeth Freestone
Literary Manager Paul Sirett
Casting Director Carrie Hilton
Casting Assistant Zara Nunn
Production Manager Julian Cree
Stage Manager Bill Foster
Assistant Stage Manager Claire Blackburn
Wardrobe Supervisor Rachel Dickson

Press Representation
Bridget Thornborrow Arts Publicity (020 7247 4437)

Advertising
Haymarket Advertising for Guy Chapman Associates

Graphic Design
Jane Harper (020 8961 0809)

Images
Stone (www.tonystone.com)

Soho Theatre and Writers' Centre
21 Dean Street, London W1D 3NE
Admin: 020 7287 5060 Fax: 020 7287 5061 Box Office: 020 7478 0100
minicom: 020 7478 0136
www.sohotheatre.com   email: mail@sohotheatre.com

Navy Pier is presented in association with Erik Lazar/Transatlantic

Navy Pier was first produced by Wax Lips Theatre Company in a different version October 1997 at Strawdog Theater, Chicago, Illinois.

MARTIN	Brendan Hunt
LIV	Anita Deely
IRIS	Ericka Kreutz
KURT	Kurt Reynolds

Directed by Joshua Neds-Fox
Set and Lighting Design by John C. Stark

The production then moved to the Live Bait Theater, Chicago, Illinois, in January, 1998, with the following change:

IRIS   Kat McDonnell

For Wax Lips Theatre Company

THE COMPANY

Paloma Baeza *Iris*

Theatre includes: Flight Into Egypt (Hampstead Theatre). Paloma has played starring roles in film including All Forgotten; Sunburn (to be released); A Connecticut Yankee in King Arthur's Court. Television includes: Far From the Madding Crowd; Anna Karenina for Channel 4 and most recently Rebel Heart for the BBC (to be shown later this year).

Joseph May *Martin*

Joe trained at the London Academy of Music and Dramatic Art. Theatre includes: Action (Theatre Nation); Lakeboat (Lyric Studio and Edinburgh Festival); Macbeth (Vital Stages) and Aunt Dan and Lemon (Almeida). Film includes: Fairy Tale—A True Story (Paramount); Wilde (Samuelson Film) and Investigating Sex (Gemini). Television includes: Casualty (BBC); Bugs (Carnival Films); Who Dares Wins (Pozzitiv TV) and A Dinner with Herbs (Festival Film and TV).

Oliver Milburn *Kurt*

Theatre includes: The Day I Stood Still and John Gabriel Borkman (Royal National Theatre); Total Eclipse (Greenwich) and The Flag (Bridge Lane). Film includes: Toothache; Paranoid; The Browning Version; Loaded and Sweet Angel Mine. Television includes: Tess of the D'Urbervilles; Families and Medics (Granada); David Copperfield; The Choir; Backup and In Your Dreams (BBC); Bright Hair (Monogram Productions for BBC) and Love in the Twenty First Century (Channel 4).

Doraly Rosen *Liv*

Recent theatre work includes Other People at the Royal Court Theatre, and productions of Macbeth and Sunshine at the Southwark Playhouse. Recent TV credits include a semi- regular character in Casualty, Kavanagh QC and The Alchemist.

John Corwin *Writer*

John is a graduate of Illinois State University and this year is one of 6 playwrights on the Soho Theatre Company's unique Writers' Attachment Programme. Plays: Slim Just Left Town (1996); Navy Pier (1997); What Does That Mean? (1998) and Gone Home (1999), for which he received the Joseph Jefferson Citation nomination for Best New Work.

Abigail Morris *Director*

Artistic Director of Soho Theatre Company since 1992. Productions include Stop Kiss, Be My Baby, Station, Kindertransport (at the Cockpit, West End and at the Manhattan Theatre Club, New York), Rock Station and Tulip Futures. Additional credits include founder and Artistic Director of Trouble and Strife Theatre Company and Noyes Fludde (Albert Hall), Julius Caesar Jones (Sadler's Wells) and Leave it to Me (Arts Theatre).

Tessa Walker *Assistant Director*

Productions include The Watched (Bedlam Theatre Company of Cornwall); Believe (The Man in the Moon Theatre, London); co-director of The Trial (Tabard Theatre); The Supposed Person (Le Petit Herbertot, Paris) and Hysteric Studs (BAC and as part of the Britannic Theatre Season at Theater Lab, Houston).

Jonathan Fensom *Designer*

Trained Trent Polytechnic. Productions for Soho Theatre Company include Stop Kiss; Be My Baby and Angels and Saints and 5 Plays: 4 Weeks (Pleasance Theatre). Other work includes: The Erpingham Camp (Edinburgh Festival and on tour); Alarms & Excursions (Producciones Alejandro Romay, Argentina); Blithe Spirit, A Streetcar Named Desire, and Richard III (Mercury Theatre, Colchester); East (Vaudeville and UK Tour); and Backroom (Bush). Jonathan was also Associate Designer on Disney's The Lion King (New Amsterdam Theatre, Broadway, Lyceum London).

Jason Taylor *Lighting Designer*

Productions for Soho Theatre Company include Stop Kiss; Be My Baby and Angels and Saints; Jump Mr Malinoff, Jump; 4 Plays: 4 Weeks; 5 Plays: 4 Weeks (Pleasance Theatre); Site Specific; Kindertransport and Tulip Futures. Other designs include 8 seasons at the Open Air Theatre, Regent's Park; Rosencrantz and Guildenstern are Dead (Piccadilly); And Then There Were None (Duke of York's); 30 productions at Nottingham Playhouse and The Emaginator, Trocadero.

soho
theatre + writers' centre

'the first new theatre in the West End for decades is an inspiration'

The Sunday Times

Soho Theatre + Writers' Centre is the new, permanent home of Soho Theatre Company who began nurturing new plays and new writers nearly 30 years ago.

The building includes a comfortable, air-conditioned theatre a studio and rehearsal room and also, uniquely, space for writers – individual rooms to work in and facilities for seminars and workshops – alongside, on the ground floor, the award-winning bar and restaurant Cafe Lazeez.

Hiring the Theatre

Soho Theatre and Writers' Centre has a range of rooms which are available for hire. Please call 0207 287 5060 or email hires@sohotheatre.com for further details.

Bars and Restaurant

Gordon's®

The main theatre bar is located in Café Lazeez Brasserie on the Ground Floor.

The Gordon's® Terrace serves Gordon's® Gin and Tonic and a range of soft drinks.

Reservations for the Café Lazeez restaurant can be made on 020 7434 9393.

Free Mailing List

Join our mailing list by contacting the Box Office on 020 7478 0100 or email us at mail@sohotheatre.com for regular online information.

Soho Theatre + Writers' Centre at 21 Dean Street, W1

the venue…

'the creative hotbed that is the revived Soho Theatre and Writers'
Centre'
The Times

'inspired…a serious success story'
The Independent

'Soho Theatre's exhilarating new home'
The Independent

'a glittering new theatre in Dean Street'
The Times

'new writing is sexy again'
Plays International

opening season spring 2000

'the delightful new Soho Theatre has justly caught the public's imagination'
Jane Edwardes, Time Out (Be My Baby)

'a great find brings new theatre to life'
Charles Spencer, Daily Telegraph (Jump, Mr Malinoff, Jump)

'if I had to pigeonhole a Soho play, I would say that they often see the
extraordinary in the ordinary, the diamonds in the dirt. None more so than
these two plays'
Lyn Gardner, The Guardian (Be My Baby & Angels and Saints)

'poetry and pathos…wonderfully funny…makes the heart expand and
crack'
Kate Stratton, Time Out (Jump, Mr Malinoff, Jump)

'tender, compassionate and sincere'
Michael Billington, The Guardian (Stop Kiss)

'if this play were a person you would want to hold it and hug it'
Lyn Gardner, The Guardian (Be My Baby)

'Be My Baby is a gem of a play'
Charles Spencer, The Daily Telegraph

'Stop Kiss brings the Soho Theatre Company's opening season to a fine
and moving climax'
Jeremy Kingston, The Times

Soho Theatre Company

Artistic Director: Abigail Morris
PA to Artistic Director: Zara Nunn

Administrative Producer: Mark Godfrey
PA to Administrative Producer: Nicole Charalambous

Literary Manager: Paul Sirett
Literary Officer: Sara Murray
Associate Director: Jonathan Lloyd
Artistic Associate: Mark Brickman
Workshop Officers: Lin Coghlan (part-time), Lisa Goldman (part-time)

Development Director: Carole Winter
Development Officer: Zoe Reed

Marketing Manager: Louise Chantal
Press Officer: Angela Dias
PR For Navy Pier: Bridget Thornborrow
BThornborrow@aol.com (020 7247 4437)

Financial Director: Kevin Dunn
Administrator: Becky Shaw
Theatre Manager: Catherine Thornborrow
Acting Theatre Managers: James Neville, Anne Moseley
Box Office/Receptionists: Alexandra Billington, Davina Whitten

Production Manager: Julian Cree
Technical Stage Managers: Claire Blackburn, Nick Blount, Bill Foster
and Jonathan Rouse.

THE SOHO THEATRE DEVELOPMENT CAMPAIGN

Soho Theatre Company gratefully acknowledges core funding from Westminster City Council and London Arts Board. However, in order to provide as diverse a programme as possible and expand our audience development and outreach work, we rely upon additional support. Many projects are only made possible by sponsorship and support from trusts, foundations and individuals.

In 2000, we launched our Writers' Attachment Programme with inaugural support from an anonymous donor. The Harold Hyam Wingate Foundation will support this vital scheme for the next three years. Sainsbury's Checkout Theatre is sponsoring the new production *Play to Win* for 10-14 year olds and Bridge House Estates Trust Fund is supporting our Access Programme.

The **New Voices** annual membership scheme is for people who care about new writing and the future of theatre. There are various levels to suit all – for further information, please visit our website at **www.sohotheatre.com/newvoices**

If you would like to help, or have any questions, please contact the development department on 020 7287 5060 or at **development@sohotheatre.com**

We are grateful to all of our sponsors and donors for their support and commitment.

PROGRAMME SUPPORTERS

Supported by **Bloomberg**

Research & Development: Anon · Samuel Goldwyn Foundation · Harold Hyam Wingate Foundation

Education: Delfont Foundation · Follett Trust · Hyde Park Place Estate Charity · Roger Jospé · Sainsbury's Checkout Theatre

Access: Bridge House Estates Trust Fund

New Voices:

Gold Patrons: Anon · Julie & Robert Breckman · David Day · Madeleine Hamel · Patrick Marber · Krister Rindell · Christian Roberts · Stagecoach Theatre Arts School (Chigwell)

Silver Patrons: Rob Brooks · Jonathan & Jacqueline Gestetner

Bronze Patrons: Davina & Larry Belling · John Drummond · Audrey & Geoffrey Morris · Alexander S. Rosen & Armand Azoulay · Nathan Silver · Paul & Pat Zatz

SOHO THEATRE + WRITERS' CENTRE

In 1996, Soho Theatre Company was awarded an £8 million Lottery grant from the Arts Council of England to help create the Soho Theatre + Writers' Centre. An additional £2.6 million in matching funds was raised and over 500 donors supported the capital appeal. The full list of supporters is displayed on our website at: **www.sohotheatre.com/ thanks.htm**

BUILDING SUPPORTERS

Supported by the Arts Council of England with National Lottery funds.

The Lorenz Auditorium supported by Carol and Alan Lorenz.

Principal sponsor: stone

Rooms: Gordon's® Terrace supported by Gordon's® Gin • The Education and Development Studio supported by the Foundation for Sport and the Arts • Equity Trust Fund Green Room • The Vicky Arenson Writers' Seminar Room • Writers' Room supported by The Samuel Goldwyn Foundation • Unity Theatre Writers' Room • Writers' Room supported by Nick Hornby and Annette Lynton Mason • The Marchpole Dressing Room • Wardrobe supported by Angels the Costumiers • The Peter Sontar Production Office • The White Light Control Room • The Strand Dimmer Room • The Dennis Selinger Meeting Room

Principal trusts and foundations: The Esmée Fairbairn Charitable Trust • LWT Award • The Pilgrim Trust • Peggy Ramsay Foundation • The Rayne Foundation • Garfield Weston Foundation • The Harold Hyam Wingate Foundation

Platinum supporters: Simon Catt at Berger Oliver • Derek and Margaret Coe • The Meckler Foundation • Roberta Sacks

Trusts and foundations: Anonymous • The Andersen Consulting Foundation • The Arts Foundation • Briess Family Charitable Trust • Mrs EE Brown Charitable Settlement • The John S Cohen Foundation • The Delfont Foundation • The Dent Charitable Trust • Claire and Michael Eisenthal Foundation • The Follett Trust • The Cecil Gee Charitable Trust • The Hon Clive and Mrs Gibsons Charitable Trust • N and J Greenwood Charitable Trust • Hyde Park Place Estate Charity • The Kirschel Foundation • Joseph Levy Charitable Foundation • The Mercers' Company • Victor Mishcon Charitable Trust • Peter Moores Foundation • The Rose Foundation • The Jacob Rothschild Charitable

John Davies • Henry and Suzanne Davis • Amanda Eliasch • Susan Ensign • Helen Fielding • Michael Frayn • Susan Frewin • Liz and Rowland Gee • Nigel Gee • Pam and Keith Gems • Anthony Georgiadis • Lord and Lady Hanson • Maurice and Irene Hatter • Tony Haygarth • Peter Hodes • Mandy Isaacs • Angela Jackson • Roslyn and Stephen Kalman • Tim and Kit Kemp • Jeremy King and Debra Hauer • Lionel and Sheila King Lassman • Peter and Lesley King-Lewis • Jonathan and Debbie Klein • Helen Kokkinou • Sara and David Kyte • Hugh and Stecia Laddie • Andria and Jonathan Lass • Colin Leventhal and Trea Hoving • Adele and Geoffrey Lewis • Lipitch Family • Paul and Paula Marber • Anthony and Pauline Margo • Valerie and Daniel Martineau • Martin and Jennifer Melman • Mark Mishon • Philip Mishon OBE and Judith Mishon • Lily and Martin Mitchell • Audrey and Geoffrey Morris • Stephen Murray • Madelaine Newton and Kevin Whately • Ossey Osmond and Roni Kermode • Joel and Merle Osrin • David Pelham • Michael Pemberton Jnr • Terence Pentony • Jill and Robin Phillips • Piper Smith & Basham • Alexander S Rosen and Armand Azoulay • Philippe Sands • Greta Scacchi • Eric and Linda Senat • John Sessions • Ingrid Simler and John Bernstein • Charlie and Jacqui Spicer • Howard Strowman • Clive Swift • Dan Tana • Norma and Brian Taylor • AP Watt Ltd • Sarah and Peter Wenban • Valerie West • Michael and Gerti Wilford • Marilyn and Geoffrey Wilson • Michael Winner Ltd • Jeremy Zimmermann

Registered Charity: 267234

CAFÉ LAZEEZ

Best Indian Restaurant 1996 & 1998
The Carlton London Restaurant Awards

Situated below the Soho Theatre, Café Lazeez
is the perfect venue for pre and post theatre dining.

Brasserie pre-theatre menu: 2 courses £7.50

Restaurant post-theatre menu: 2 courses £12.50

'*A sophisticated restaurant with great food*'   Harpers & Queen

'*Café Lazeez offers fine Indian dining*'   The Guardian Guide

'*Spice it up... Café Lazeez is perfect if you fancy an Indian
but your friends want burgers or pasta*'   The Sunday Times

Café Lazeez
21 Dean Street, Soho, London
RESERVATIONS: 020 7434 9393
Open Daily Mon-Sat 11.00 am-1.00 am
& Sunday 12 noon-10.30 pm

First published in 2000 by Oberon Books Ltd.
(incorporating Absolute Classics)
521 Caledonian Road, London N7 9RH
Tel: 020 7607 3637 / Fax: 020 7607 3629
e-mail: oberon.books@btinternet.com

A catalogue record for this book is available from the British Library.

ISBN: 1 84002 199 3

Cover design: Humphrey Gudgeon

Series design: Richard Doust

Printed in Great Britain by Antony Rowe Ltd, Reading.

Characters

MARTIN

LIV

IRIS

KURT

LIV, MARTIN, IRIS and KURT. They talk to the audience, occasionally to each other.

MARTIN: My name is Martin. *Martin.*

LIV: My name is Olivia. But everyone just calls me Liv.

IRIS: My name is Iris. After my mother's mother.

KURT: Kurt.

Pause.

MARTIN: Ah. I love this city. San Francisco. It's beautiful. I love all the hills especially. I know, it's the first thing anyone ever says about San Francisco. 'Ooooh, the *hills.*' But still…so damn hilly. At least in comparison to Chicago. Which of course is quite flat.

Pause.

And it's not just the hills. No. There's the ocean just to the west. There's the bay. And, of course, there's the fog. Every morning the fog rolls in from the ocean. Right before dawn. Like clockwork. I love the way it… consumes everything. Unstoppable. Enveloping everything in its path. It's hypnotic. One minute, a building or a…landmark is there, the next minute, gone.

Pause.

My favorite is Alcatraz. Watching Alcatraz disappear.

Pause.

You should try it sometime. Wake up before dawn and watch the fog roll in from the ocean.

LIV: Never stayed in a hotel before. For such an extended period of time. Five days now. The Hotel Edison.

Pause.

It's nice. Fresh towels every day, sheets. Room service. Cable. All that. It even has a kitchenette. I like it.

Pause.

But I don't know. Maybe it's the way they try to make it comfortable for you, you know, 'Just Like Home'. The paintings on the wall, the furniture that almost matches, but doesn't. The more they try, the more you realise you're not home, you're only here temporarily. Odd. It constantly reminds you of where you aren't.

Pause.

And as a result, I find myself thinking about home a lot. That apartment. Missing it.

Pause.

Homesickness. Pure and simple.

MARTIN: And you should also meet my…you should meet Olivia. Everyone just calls her Liv, so…

Pause.

She's…she's…phenomenal. Truly. She is the Cat's Pajamas, she is the Bee's Knees. I met her soon after I moved to San Francisco. The bar she used to work at. She's…the most beautiful woman I have ever met. She denies it, of course. She feels she's run of the mill, but…that's just her way.

Pause.

She's been gone for a while now, but…she will return soon. From wherever she is. I am confident of that. Yes.

Pause.

I mean: she can't stay gone forever, right? Right.

IRIS: I have been back in Chicago for eight months now. A sort of homecoming. Went to college here. But…that seems such a long time ago. When I first moved back here, I walked around. The old haunts. All my friends, the people I knew back then have gone, and I do not know how to find them. There is no one here who knows me. Except for myself. I am the only one who knows me.

Pause. She smiles.

And sometimes I wonder about that.

KURT: I cannot write when the sun is up – I do my *best* work at night – So I have adjusted my life accordingly. I get up around noon. Go out. Wander around, see what's what. Come home around nine, *then* I can start writing. Work on that until about four or five in the morning. Go to sleep. Do the whole thing over again the next day.

Pause.

Every so often, I forget what day it is, I have to ask someone, but I don't care. Because I am contented, you see, and how many of us can say that?

IRIS: I have a good job, though, so *that* helps. I teach. Art. To seventh-graders. On the North Side. I like it more than I thought I would. There is one girl, her name is Maura. Especially talented. I am amazed by some of the work she is doing– She's only *twelve* – She likes to paint. It gives her great satisfaction. And she could be so good. If she kept at it.

Pause. She smiles.

But…she's just starting to discover Boys. So…

Pause.

My social life has been…streamlined, so to speak. A lot of time to think. How I came to be here. Now.

MARTIN: I was nervous coming out here. And it was rough going at first – I had…moments. Episodes – But that is perfectly normal and to be expected. You know. Nothing wrong with needing a little…adjustment period. I mean, after all, I certainly would have needed adjustment after…

Silence. He smiles.

And so I get that great view of the bay. When I get up in the morning, I sit and look out the window. Fog rolls in, comes out of nowhere, it goes on its devouring path. I count the seconds it takes for the buildings to vanish. One…two…three…four…

LIV: It was so quiet in that apartment. The last few weeks. I would walk down the hall, past his study. First thing in the morning, he'd be in there.
'Martin? What do you wanna do today? I don't have to work, so we have the whole day together.'

Pause.

'Martin? *Helloooo?*'

MARTIN: Nineteen…twenty…twenty-one…twenty-two…

LIV: It was strange. And it happened overnight. He just stopped leaving his room. I didn't see him, couldn't talk to him.

Pause.

And then, once he *left* the room…well…

Pause.

My friends would ask me what was wrong, why was I upset. And I could only say: 'What do you want to hear? Where do I begin?'
'Begin at the beginning,' they'd say. 'Just begin at the beginning.' Which is what I'll do.

IRIS: *Yes. Do that.*

MARTIN: (*Holding newspaper.*) Here. Did you see this? Did you read this? Here: Listen to this:

Pause.

'*The Splits* is astonishing. This novel clearly announces Kurt Mitchell as a writer whose voice demands attention.'

'Whose voice demands attention.' Hah.

'A book that grabs you, refuses to let go. The literary equivalent of a knockout punch.'

Pause.

Can you believe that? That fucking shit? I mean…ah.

KURT: Well. I was wondering how long it'd take before he mentioned me.

Pause.

Don't believe everything you hear about me, by the way.

MARTIN: He taught me everything I knew. Everything I know now. Kurt Mitchell. It's just that simple.

Pause.

We were in college together. Two English majors.

IRIS: Me, I was an Art major.

LIV: American History. 1865-Present. At the University of San Francisco, though.

MARTIN: *Fine, good.* But Kurt and I were English majors. And what we would do is walk all over campus. That's how we'd pass the time. Walking all over Chicago; all damn day – By the end of the year, there was actually definition in my leg muscles. You could see *calves.*

Pause.

We'd talk about whatever, you know. Whatever mattered then. Whatever was affecting our lives in the present. Things like…

Pause.

Like…

Pause.

KURT: Like Women.

MARTIN: Like *Women.* Holy Christ, *yes.* We talked of women. Who we wanted, who was catching our eye, who was clouding our minds – *And they always cloud your minds, don't they?* – Ah. Women.

Pause.

All this, of course, is before I met Iris. Understand that. *And it was…good, wasn't it?*

IRIS: *Most certainly was.*

MARTIN: *Better than good, in fact.* And it always seemed to be him. Kurt. Giving me advice. Listening to my thoughts, my doubts. Telling me how to proceed. Because I was so clueless. Really. I was. Without a clue.

Pause.

I often thought, Here is a man in control. Because he always seemed so sure of himself. At parties. Attracting women at will. In class, speaking articulately about his work and that of others. He was so…adaptable. To whatever situation. He was comfortable. At ease. Yes.

Pause.

He put me to shame.

Pause.

But I was never jealous of him. Not at all. But I must say that I did…observe him. See why he was so successful in all those situations. What about him, his fabric, made him so at ease, gave him that air of confidence. I tried to learn from him. See what I could glean from him.

Pause.

Of course I could never approach his status. Not a chance in hell. How could I? I mean: he is he and I am me, and there is only one of him and there is only one of me. You see? But…I tried. I really tried.

IRIS: I watched him trying and I did understand, but still…I tried to tell him, make him see, that he had good qualities of his own. And that he should just be himself. All anyone can do. But I don't think I ever got through to him. And eventually…well.

Pause.

We would go to parties. Bars. You know…*college.* We'd see Kurt. And whoever was with him. Each week, a different woman. And it is true: there was something about him. I won't deny it. You could just tell. People always knew where he was, wherever he was. And… Kurt knew it. The effect he had on people. Was in his eyes.

Pause.

I would watch Martin watching Kurt. From across the room.

MARTIN: 'Look. How easy it is for him.'

IRIS: And I looked. Watched Kurt.

Pause.

I found myself watching him more and more.

MARTIN: And then, of course, after the walks, we'd go
  play...*air hockey.*

IRIS: I played air hockey once.

KURT: *Hah.* I'd nearly forgotten.

LIV: Don't think I ever played it.

MARTIN: There were pinball and video games, of course.
  But we had no use for them. No. It was air hockey for
  us. We'd play for hours. At first, it was quite friendly.
  But...eventually we had to keep track of who was
  winning more games. And that sure made things
  interesting. The friendly insults, the bragging, they were
  gone as we stood there, facing off against one another.
  Not saying a word. Letting the game itself say
  everything. Sure, he held an edge at first. But...I'd like
  to think that I got better as the years progressed. I think
  we were about even by the time we graduated. Yes.
  I was at least as good as him. I think we were equals.
  I really do.

  Pause.

LIV: The first time I saw Martin. San Francisco. I had just
  graduated, but...hard to find a job, History degree.
  So...while I was sending out resumes, interviewing,
  I picked up some shifts at this bar down the hill. Bigsby's.

  Pause.

  Anyway. The first time I saw him. Saturday night. Nine
  o'clock. The bar was dead. Only seven or eight people
  in the whole place. He came in. Sat at a corner stool.

MARTIN: 'Can I get a Harp?'

LIV: He sat there. Completely alone. He went through two
  Harps. I thought: 'How sad.' Sitting at a bar alone on a
  Saturday night. I went back to the kitchen, get some

limes. Came back out front. And…he was sitting at this table with five women. And they all seemed to be quite taken with him. Everyone was laughing. The drinks were coming round after round after round, and…I had never seen someone so confident. Really. He had…an aura.

Pause.

One of the women came to the bar, order another round. I couldn't resist myself.
'Did you know that guy?'
'Who, at the table?'
'Yes.'
'No. We just met him tonight.'
'All of you did? He was a complete stranger?'
'Yes.'

Pause.

Unbelievable.

Pause.

And when it was time to close up shop, long after they were the only ones left in the place, one of the girls – *the prettiest one, if you ask me* – invited him back to her place. 'To talk.' – *Right* – And…at first, he begged off. Seemed a little scared, actually. Which surprised me. But then, he…well, it's like he composed himself.

MARTIN: 'I'd love to go back to your place. And…talk some more.'

LIV: And off they went.

Pause.

I went to the window. Watched them walk down the street. Disappear into the fog.
'Boy did I underestimate that one.'

Pause.

MARTIN: And then, after we were done with the air
hockey, we'd go to the coffeeshop just across the street.
That's where we'd finish our day. Had our own table.
Sit there, drink coffee. Show each other what we'd
written. We were writing like madmen then. So much
energy. It was our own little workshop. An open and
honest exchange. I showed him everything I wrote.
Without hesitation. Even as I kept everything from Iris.
Because I trusted him completely.

Pause.

Now: I know you should never trust anyone more than
you trust yourself, but…I was so in awe of him. Wanted
so much to be viewed as his equal, his peer…

Pause.

And I listened to him. Everything he told me.

KURT: 'Find your own voice.'

MARTIN: That's what he said to me. A Tuesday afternoon
in February. In the coffeeshop.

KURT: 'Find your own voice.'

Pause.

Because that's what I thought he needed to do.

MARTIN: So that's what I did, that's what I worked on –
Even though I never really knew what that meant.

IRIS: And so, without warning, he was always writing.
Martin. Always in that lousy, little coffeeshop. It was as
if I became…a secondary concern. I actually saw him,
actually spent time with him maybe once a week. And
even then, it was: 'So. What are you working on, that
I see you in the coffeeshop all day?'

MARTIN: 'Oh, nothing.'

IRIS: 'Nothing? Awfully busy for a guy working on nothing.'

MARTIN: 'Ah. Nothing worth showing anyone.'

IRIS: 'I'd really like to read it, hon.'

MARTIN: 'Not yet.'

IRIS: End of conversation. That's how it was for the last four months. Until school ended…and the three of us…graduated. Maybe go out once a week. The rest of the time, him scribbling at the kitchen table. Me, painting, wanting to show it to him, hoping he'd ask me to – *because he used to take an interest.*

Pause.

You see, we used to talk. I used to be…happy. For two years. It's important that you understand that.
But then…to be…pushed aside…
Well…

She looks at KURT, who smiles.

KURT: I find myself rather suddenly of the age where I check a woman's ring finger to see if she's married – or engaged – before I proceed. Getting old or something. Used to think that it'd never happen to me.

Pause.

Sat in the bookstore the other day. Looked at the copies of my book on the display – Of course no one was even scanning over them – So I just watched all the women who passed by. Brunettes. You know I have a thing for brunettes.

MARTIN: I always had a thing for redheads. He always had a predilection for brunettes. Yep.

Pause.

Only the *occasional* redhead for him.

KURT: And I looked at them. Wondering if they were spoken for. And wouldn't you know it, more often than not, they were.

Pause.

And I would catch myself fantasising about them. And no, it wasn't sex fantasies. Please. I've *never* had to fantasise about sex. No. I thought about…what it would be like with them in my life. To be a part of their lives.

Pause.

I never approach them. The women who obviously are spoken for. I keep my safe distance. Please. Give me some credit.

Pause.

But sometimes, they approach me. Yes. Sometimes they make that first move. And when that happens, well… what's a boy to do.

Pause. He smiles, looks at IRIS, who looks away. Pause.

LIV: Martin didn't come into the bar for six or seven months after that. Until spring. The woman would come in every other night or so. Looking for him. Sometimes, she'd sit on his corner stool all night, waiting for him. But he never showed up. And eventually the woman stopped coming in.

Pause.

And so, spring came, one night, he just showed up.

MARTIN: 'Can I get a Harp?'

LIV: He sat at the corner stool. It was another slow night. So I started talking to him. See if I could get that aura again. 'Hi.'

MARTIN: 'Hi.'

LIV: 'My name's Liv.'

Pause.

Something in his eyes, what *is* that?

MARTIN: 'My name's Kurt.'

LIV: 'Nice to meet you.'

MARTIN: 'Nice to meet *you.*'

Pause. They smile. Pause.

LIV: And that's how it started. With that introduction.

We talked all night. I talked a lot. Which is rare.

Pause.

At the end of the night:

MARTIN: 'Can I see you again?'

LIV: 'Hey. I'm here every Friday, Saturday and Sunday.
All you have to do is show up, buy a beer…'

MARTIN: 'No. Away from here. On a date.'

LIV: 'Ah. I see.' – *Well, what the hell, I didn't get out enough
anyway, right?*

So we made plans for the next Thursday. He kissed my
cheek as he left.

Pause.

He never showed up, supposed to be there at eight,
I waited until nine-thirty. Which I think was more than
giving him the benefit of the doubt. So I went home.

Pause.

He came into the bar the next night. Looking quite ill.
He said he was very sorry, but he lied to me. The whole

last Saturday was a lie and he didn't want to continue with the lie, and if we were going to go on, he would have to set the record straight. I didn't have a clue what he was talking about. Found out soon enough.

MARTIN: 'My name is not Kurt. It's Martin.'

Pause.

LIV: 'Okay.' *What the hell do you say...?*

Pause.

IRIS: It was Monday, April fifteenth. Walking home, past the coffeeshop, Martin wasn't in there, where could he be? Kurt was in there. I went in. 'Know where Martin is?'

KURT: 'I don't know. Haven't seen him all day.'

IRIS: *Great.*

Pause.

I got some coffee, sat down with Kurt. We talked for a bit. And then...

KURT: 'Hey. Let's go play some air hockey. It's right across the street.'

IRIS: Well...I had never played. But I had nothing else to do. So...why not?

Pause.

We went across the street. To the arcade. He broke a five. Got quarters. 'What are the rules?'

KURT: 'There are no rules.'

IRIS: 'There must be rules.'

KURT: 'Not the way I play.'

IRIS: He put quarters into the game, put the puck down on the surface, and it...floated. Without anyone touching it.

It...hovered, drifted to one side, from the air being forced up through those tiny holes in the surface. Bounce off the edge, come floating, drifting back. No particular hurry. Just floating.

KURT: The thing about air hockey is, and this is what's most important, is the eye contact. Don't follow the puck. Moves too fast, you could never keep up with it. No. Look at him. Look at your opponent. Then you can see which way he's going with it, you can follow the flow of the game. And, if you stick with it, if you concentrate, are aware, he'll give something away. You can detect a weakness.

MARTIN: He'd always say shit like that. Turn it into this big thing. It's fucking air hockey for chrissakes. You get the damn red puck past the other guy. That's it. No use making it more than what it is.

Pause.

And like I said, by the end, he was no better than me. No better.

KURT: And the flipside of that, just as important, make sure *your* eyes reveal nothing to your opponent. Keep your true intentions hidden.

MARTIN: *Pfff.*

KURT: 'You ready?'

IRIS: 'Yes'.

KURT: 'Then here we go.'

IRIS: He started the game, a simple volley, we just passed the puck back and forth, back and forth, back and forth, then he slapped it hard, it caromed off the right side, right past me.

KURT: She was favouring her left. I saw this.

IRIS: I looked at him – Thought we were playing *easy* –
He grinned.

KURT: 'One-nothing.'

IRIS: I served, we volleyed again, but with a little more
purpose on my part. Again, he slapped it hard, it
caromed off the side, right past me.

KURT: Favoring her *left*.

Pause.

'Two-nothing.'

IRIS: He was really grinning now. My face was hot. I felt
flushed. Wasn't going to let that happen again. Gonna
wipe that smug little grin off his face. It was his serve, he
floated it out there, and I slapped it right past him. Bam.

KURT: 'What the...'

IRIS: I grinned at *him* this time. 'Two-*one*.' It was my serve.
Faked left, shot right, bam again. 'Two-*two*.'

KURT: She was much quicker than Martin ever was. Much.

IRIS: And the game was on. He hunkered down, put on his
'game face'.

KURT: 'No more playing around with you.'

IRIS: 'Good. Wouldn't want you going easy on me.'

Pause.

He was trying to look cool but he was a little flushed
now, too. Straining. Which was good. I wanted him to
try. Because I was going to try my best to beat him. And
I would. I was going to win. Just a matter of time. *And
quarters.*

LIV: Martin said he was very sorry but he lied to me, about
who he was, and he didn't want to lie to me or to

anyone else anymore about who he was, and if I gave him just half a chance, he'd never lie to me again, about anything, and I would never regret it.

Pause.

This *guy*…

MARTIN: *I don't know.*

LIV: Everything in me told me to just walk away, forget the whole thing. But…there was something about him…

Pause.

So I told him I would think about it. You know. And he said he understood. And after that, he would come into the bar once a day. Hand me a manila envelope. And then he would walk out the door. Without a word.

Pause.

And inside the envelope was…a story, I guess. Or a poem. Little paragraph. Whatever. Each day it was something different.

MARTIN: The first time I had written in…many, many months.

LIV: He wasn't trying to 'woo' me. He was just trying to…let me know who he was. Or who he might be.

Pause.

And on Fridays, after I had been off work for four days, he would bring in four envelopes. It got to be so that Friday was my favorite day, four envelopes, four slips of paper – My favorite one was only four words long, centered in the page. 'I love your hips.' Imagine that. Someone loving these hips.

Pause.

So anyway. It lasted four weeks. Until I finally gave in.

Agreed to go out with him again. Or for the first time.

Pause.

And, as it turned out, we had a great time. Great.

IRIS: We played air hockey for six hours, Kurt and me. Fierce competition. The whole time I felt as if I were… outside myself, beyond myself. I was energised. And I had him on the ropes at the end.

KURT: I don't think so.

IRIS: I really did. He was reeling, his timing was just a hair off. We squared off there at the end, neither one of us speaking, neither one of us looking at the other – He gave that up after the third game, *hah* – There was only the puck, that red disk. That's all that mattered.

Pause.

The final tally was fifteen games for him; eleven for me.

Pause.

I must say that he was a very gracious winner. Half expected him to gloat, you know, make sure I know who won, but there was none of that.

KURT: 'You did better than Martin usually does.'

Pause.

Which was the truth.

IRIS: Which I suspected was a lie. But I let it pass. It was ten-thirty.

KURT: 'What do you say we go get a beer?' – I was… thirsty.

IRIS: 'Sounds like a good idea.' We went to a bar around the corner.

MARTIN: Alright, can I say something here, please?

IRIS: We sat in silence at first, just drank the beers.

KURT: Four dollar pitchers were the special. Every Monday night.

IRIS: Finally…he went into his bag.

KURT: 'Let me show you something.'

MARTIN: No.

IRIS: He rummaged around, pulled out a black binder.

KURT: 'I want you to read this.'

IRIS: Handed it to me. I opened the binder.

MARTIN: *Isaac Greets the New Day.*

KURT: By Kurt Mitchell.

MARTIN: *Ah.*

IRIS: He said he sent it off to *The New Yorker* that morning.

KURT: 'Just hope it's good enough.'

IRIS: I started to read it right there. Which was a mistake. Should have read it when he wasn't sitting right across the booth. When I finished, I didn't know what to say. 'I don't know what to say.'

KURT: 'Did you like it?'

IRIS: 'Yes. Very much. I…'

Pause.

'You were right to send it out.'

KURT: 'Thank you.'

IRIS: 'You're welcome.'

Pause.

KURT: 'You know…I wrote it for you.'

MARTIN: *Oh for the love of…*

IRIS: No one ever said that to me before. Martin never even let me *read* anything of his.

KURT: 'I'm sorry. I shouldn't be doing this to you…telling you this.'

IRIS: *It's alright. I want to hear it.*

KURT: 'I just…I…you've been on my mind. And…well, you just read what comes of that.'

IRIS: *Oh God, I shouldn't be here, I should get the HELL out of here, right now.* But I stayed.

MARTIN: No.

IRIS: I mean: it should have been Martin who was writing these words for me. That's what I really wanted. Not him, not Kurt. But…Martin wasn't there. Now…I am not palming this off on Martin. We are all complicitous. Yes. Much of the blame lies with me.

Pause.

So I stayed. I looked at him. He looked at me.

KURT: Never noticed how beautiful she was. Beautiful red hair.

IRIS: *My face feels hot; hope I'm not blushing.* He slid his hand across the table. It touched mine. I held it. *Oh God oh God oh God, I know where this is going.* And then he asked me if I wanted to go back to his apartment.

KURT: No. I didn't.

Pause.

IRIS: *What?*

KURT: *Let's get it right, shall we? She* asked *me.* If we could go back to my place. She asked me.

IRIS: *No. I didn't. You...*

KURT: Don't get me wrong. I was gonna ask her. Was building to that all night. But she beat me to it. Took the bull by the horns. As it were.

Pause. IRIS looks away.

KURT: That's right.

Pause.

MARTIN: So sometimes, and this is way back in college, in Chicago, before I moved here to San Francisco, sometimes, I'd try to write and...Nothing. Would. Happen.

Pause.

So I would walk the streets. Trying to get some kinda...inspiration, I guess.

KURT: 'Find your own voice.'

MARTIN: That's what he said to me.

KURT: 'Find your own voice.'

MARTIN: Yep. Just like that.

Pause.

And that was what I was doing. At the expense of everything else.

Pause.

But I felt it was worth it. Worth the risk.

Pause.

So I would walk.

Pause.

And one Monday night, I was out walking. I was trying to write, and…nothing. A blank. But this time, it was worse than the others, because I must say I had been in a bit of a groove. But there I was, stuck again. So… walking, drifting along, this brilliant starlit night. Cursing myself. But, after a few hours, I began to calm down, get a little perspective, healthier outlook, maybe even a smile on my face.

Pause.

And of course, then it started to rain.

Pause.

Luckily, I was near his apartment. I ran for two blocks. I took a left. Ran for another block. Almost there. Almost safe. I took a right. And that's when I saw…her car.

Pause.

I looked in his window. First floor, second from the right. The shade was down. But the lights were on inside. I saw what was happening.

IRIS: Whether I asked him, or he asked me, whatever, we wound up at Kurt's apartment. Okay? That's what's important. We were there. Very late. And we're all adults here, aren't we? I don't have to go into what happened. Or how many *times.* It's not necessary.

Pause.

I finally left his apartment at four. It was pouring rain. He walked me to my car. Him in his robe and Birkenstocks. Under an umbrella. Hair all messed. What a *sight.* He kissed me goodbye. *I still didn't entirely want to go.*

Pause.

I drove around for an hour. Rehearsing my story, trying to get it right, be calm. Finally I worked up my courage. Walked in the door.

Pause.

Martin had no idea. *How could he?* He was scribbling away at that kitchen table. Scribble, scribble, scribble. He didn't even ask me where I was. He looked at me for a long time when I walked in, though. But he said nothing.

Pause.

I wondered if he even knew I had been out.

Pause.

LIV: We saw a lot of each other after that first date. When I was working, Martin'd sit at the bar scribbling in his notebook. And then, when I was done, we'd go to his place. He'd help me send out resumes, fill out applications. And it was…it was nice. I felt at ease, comfortable.

Pause.

IRIS: I wasn't going to keep it up for very long. With Kurt. Only wanted it to last a week or so. Just long enough to establish a tawdry little secret. But…things only accelerated. Kurt talked to me. Took an interest in what I was doing, what I thought. I walked around with the story always somewhere on my person. I kept it hidden, of course – Couldn't let Martin see it, no. So I found that I couldn't *not* think of Kurt. He was always somewhere in my mind. So for five weeks, the rest of the semester, I was at Kurt's apartment three nights a week.

Pause.

I wish I didn't enjoy it so much.

LIV: So let me explain it to you now. I have had four boyfriends – men, lovers, whatever you want to call them – In my whole life. And they were no big shakes – I mean, if you could *see* some of…But you know. I don't wish it was otherwise. Just the way it is. Until I met Martin, I had kept everyone at arm's length.

Pause.

But with Martin…

Pause.

Like I said, I was comfortable around him. So…I was staying over at his place more and more.

MARTIN: 'Big old apartment, little old me. All by my lonesome.'

LIV: And my roommate – Vivian, we were Viv and Liv – well, she didn't like Martin so much, and she could get a little…she had a streak about her. So Vivian finally calls me up one night at his place, says she wants to find a new roommate, one who'd 'be around more often.' Would I mind if she did that?

Pause.

I looked at Martin. 'Yeah. Go ahead, Viv.'

Pause.

And when I hung up the phone:

MARTIN: 'I love you. Just thought you should know that.'

LIV: The first time those words were ever said to me. *I felt my lower lip tremble.*

Pause.

'Love you, too, Martin.'

MARTIN: (*Smiling.*) 'As long as we understand one another.'

LIV: (*Smiling.*) 'I think we do.'

Pause.

So the next day, moved all my stuff into his place. And that's where I stayed. Three months after I met him. Liv was living with the guy.

Pause.

Seemed like the natural course of events.

Pause.

IRIS: And, on May sixteenth, the day after graduation, Kurt told me *The New Yorker* was going to publish *Isaac*.

KURT: '*The New Yorker* is going to publish *Isaac*.'

IRIS: 'Congratulations.'

KURT: 'I'm moving to New York. Tonight. That's the only place to be.'

Pause.

'You should come with.'

IRIS: 'What?! I can't go with you. It's impossible.'

KURT: 'Sure you can. It's easy. Just come.'

IRIS: 'Ah. I'm not so sure…'

KURT: 'Don't make me beg.'

IRIS: I'd already made up my mind. Probably made it up five weeks ago.

KURT: She practically jumped into my arms.

Pause.

LIV: The night I moved in. We had a nice dinner, Chinatown. On the way back, we stopped for chocolate ice cream. We walked past the old Chinese men doing Tai chi in the park. We walked back up the hill. Back to his apartment. He walked through the front door.
I followed.

Pause.

'This is my new home.'

MARTIN: Later, we lay in bed next to each other. I felt her tears on my shoulder. 'Liv…?' She said nothing. Just smiled. Maybe she held me a little tighter, or maybe I just imagined it.

Pause.

IRIS: I have no idea why I did it. I knew all about Kurt. Heard all the stories. Never thought it would be anything permanent. But…Besides, I saw something in him. In his eyes. Told me I'd be okay.

KURT: You can imagine my elation – Or maybe you can't. I don't know you. I got the mail at one-thirty, and there was the envelope. From *The New Yorker* offices, New York, NY. And I knew what was inside. Didn't even have to open the envelope.

Pause.

My whole life had just changed.

Pause.

Started to run to the coffeeshop, tell Martin. *Why? What could I possibly say to him?* So…I ran to his apartment instead. I knew he wouldn't be there, and for some reason I also wanted to tell her.

Pause.

'Take her with.' The first thing I thought when she opened the door. Standing there in her smock. Paint all over her. 'Take her with.'

Pause.

Now why would I do that?

IRIS: Packed my things. I left Martin a note. On the pillow. Couldn't think of much to say. *As if there was anything I could say.* So I just told him I was sorry.

Pause.

Which I was.

KURT: The next few hours I don't remember so well. I only remember sensations. Like the smell of gasoline. The taste of Coca-Cola. The feeling that no one can touch me, that I'm above it all.

Pause.

The feeling that I'm floating.

MARTIN: I stared at the note left on my pillow.

Pause.

Didn't really feel like staying in Chicago, you know, so…I tied up some loose ends, and eight days later, I was at O'Hare. United terminal. I looked at the departure board. All the cities I could go to. So many cities. And I saw one. A city I had always wanted to live in. For as long as I could remember. So I bought a ticket to San Francisco. One-way ticket.

LIV: I was frightened. In a way that I had never been frightened before. Neither one of us slept that night. We were silent. I held him, buried my face in his shoulder.

Pause.

In the morning, he didn't ask and I didn't tell him. Of my doubts. Of this uncertain feeling.

MARTIN: Oh, I knew what she was feeling. Hell, at some level, I was feeling it, too. If we're to be honest here. But, you know, you gotta take the plunge, right? Can't let a little fear stand in your way.

Pause.

That first night, I wanted to tell her of Iris and Kurt. Of all that happened back in Chicago. And how difficult my first year in San Francisco was before I met Liv.

Pause.

But maybe it didn't matter so much to me anymore. That night, as I held her, I realised that me and Liv together would be enough.

Pause.

I remember thinking that.

IRIS: We drove to New York. Packed everything into his Pontiac. Headed East. We were out of Chicago by four o'clock. I watched it fade in my side view mirror.

Pause.

His story sat in a black binder on my lap. I thumbed through it, it made me smile.

Pause.

I get sleepy when I ride in cars. So I knew it was just a matter of time. Held out as long as I could. But I fell asleep, sure enough. Somewhere in Indiana.

Pause.

Right before I fell asleep, I looked at him. His neck. His arms. I had a good feeling about this. I was tingles all over. I dunno – I guess for the first time you could call that feeling Love.

KURT: I finally calmed down once we got on the road. Thank God. Iris fell asleep like five minutes after we left. And once we left Chicago, once we got out of range, I couldn't get anything on the radio. Nothing but static. And country. So I just flipped the damn thing off. Only the sound of tyres on pavement.

Pause.

And another feeling. For the first time, there's an inkling of …what, regret?

IRIS looks at KURT. Pause.

LIV: Eventually, the doubts subsided. And then…I was in a damn near constant state of elation. I was head over heels. Hopelessly falling. I found myself talking about him. Constantly. To others. I would break out in giggles at work. Whenever anyone would order a Harp, giggling like a schoolgirl. The first few months were amazing. Absolutely. I wondered if the feeling would ever end.

Pause.

And then…sure enough…

IRIS: It took us fifteen hours to get to New York. He did most of the driving.

KURT: She drove like Willy *Loman.* Never get there the way she drove.

IRIS: And, a couple days later, we had an apartment. It wasn't much. A small little one bedroom in Brooklyn Heights. Montague Street. But it was…cosy. And it was *ours.*

KURT: It was a *pit.* Too damned small. But…I knew we'd have a much nicer place soon enough.

IRIS: All of a sudden, I was living this almost storybook life. Just Kurt and myself, in this huge new city. We spent time in Manhattan, Central Park, Greenwich Village. Holding hands, the occasional surreptitious kiss. At night, I worked at my easel in the living room; he worked on the computer in the bedroom. I felt content, I felt valued, I felt…safe.

Pause.

I began to find it harder and harder to remember what life was like in Chicago, and why I didn't miss it.

MARTIN: When I first arrived in San Francisco, I checked into a transient hotel three blocks from Chinatown. I had to share a bathroom down the hallway with seven other men. They were ugly and quite frightening, actually, these men – And the bathroom was just filthy.

Pause.

Fucking hated that hotel. Couldn't stand being in it for anything other than sleeping. So, each day, crack of dawn, I'd set out to discover something new. Learn the names of places, their histories. Or ride the trolleys all day. Or sit on a bench at the pier, and watch people. Whatever. As long as I wasn't in that room.

Pause.

So I spent my days roaming. Talking to no one. Abject silence.

Pause.

Because I knew no one. I had no one to fall back on. You see. And everywhere I went, everyone I saw, reminded me of Chicago. It wasn't a homesickness, but still. Thinking about Chicago. Mainly Kurt and Iris. And then, after a while, mainly Kurt. Air hockey. Shooting the proverbial shit. Showing each other what we were writing. He was the one I missed most.

Pause.

LIV: Okay. Here it is: There was a story Martin would read to me. It started a few months after I moved in. After dinner or sitting on the couch, he'd whip out his tattered, yellowed *New Yorker*, and read it to me. *Isaac Greets the New Day*. All eight pages. And it was…he came alive. His eyes. His whole demeanor. He would hunch over the table, over the magazine, and read it aloud. He became transformed. That may sound like an exaggeration, but it's not.

Pause.

And when he finished, he always asked me what I thought of it.

MARTIN: 'What do you think of it?'

LIV: 'It's very good.'

MARTIN: 'Yes. It's not bad, huh?'

LIV: 'No. It's quite good.'

MARTIN: 'Yes. It is. Quite good.'

    Pause.

    'I know him, you know. The guy who wrote it.'

LIV: As if I could forget he knew the author.

    Pause.

I made the mistake of talking about it to a friend. One night at the bar – don't know what I was thinking. And with a sneer: 'Good God, Liv. Don't you find that a bit…peculiar.'
'You know what, you'd never understand, so just shut the fuck up.' And she knew to shut up, because I only swear when I'm really upset.

MARTIN: And as I continued exploring, roaming, in abject silence, I began to feel better. I began to get a…grasp on things. A better handle. I even found a little coffeeshop a few blocks from the hotel. I spent a lot of time there. Trying to write. As if my friend Kurt was across the table from me.

Pause.

And one day…a breakthrough. Eleven hours in the coffeeshop, forty something pages that I was actually proud of. I got up, paid the check, and started to leave. There was a man sitting at the table by the door, reading a New Yorker, smiling. He was completely engrossed. I was curious, what's he reading. So I stopped as I passed him, looked over his shoulder. I recognised it. Whole paragraphs of it. And instantly, I thought of the coffeeshop back in Chicago. Of Kurt and I showing each other what we'd written. Yes. I recognised it from back then. So I asked the man what he was reading, just to be sure.
Isaac Greets the New Day.
Ah. Yes.
I asked him who wrote it. *Even though I knew damn well.* He flipped back a few pages. 'Kurt Mitchell. Contest winner.'
I asked him if he liked it.
'Yes, very much, it's quite good.'

Pause.

Well. He had beaten me again. Shit. And I…

Pause.

I began to shake. To weep. Got the hell out of there. As fast as I could.

Pause.

The next thing I knew, I was sitting at the pier. My toes were hanging over the edge. It was morning. I threw my pen and notebook into the bay. And I sat there wondering what I should do next.

Pause.

Wait a minute. I could reinvent myself. Because no one knew who the fuck I was. I could be whoever I wanted to be. But who?

Pause.

And then all of a sudden, it all made sense. I could be him. I could be Kurt Mitchell. Fucking brilliant.

Pause.

I stood up, and walked away, smiling perhaps the best, most confident smile of my whole life. Because no matter what was in store for me, I was sure that it was at least gonna be damn interesting, full of new discoveries and adventures.

IRIS: It was like I was reborn. I was painting furiously. More than I ever had. Ideas, pictures kept coming to me. Every time I closed my eyes. I was convinced it was my surroundings. So…twice a week, we went out, do something we'd never done before.

KURT: Two nights a week were hers. That was the agreement. Whatever she wanted to do. Just like she said, we discovered the city together.

Pause.

But the other five nights were mine and no one else's. Totally devoted to the writing. Hours at a time. I was truly happy. Sitting in my room, at the computer, knowing she was out there, painting, I suppose, happy, too. So a lot of the time, I'd just sit there, with a smile on my face, because I knew that I'd be okay.

Pause.

People would know who I was.

MARTIN: It was better, more liberating than I dared hope. I was starting from scratch. I had a name, someone to emulate, and...faith. I was unstoppable. I carried myself with an air that can best be described as exuberant. My stride had more purpose. My eyes had more focus, had a glint. And I saw that people noticed this. I was treated with...respect. It was as if it were second nature to me – As I imagine it must be for him. I was finally who I wanted to be.

Pause.

So it went on like this. For some time. A few months. This feeling that I could not be stopped. And one night, one Saturday night, I went to this corner bar down the hill. Bigsby's.

LIV: The first night I saw him.

MARTIN: I went into the bar at nine-thirty. 'Can I get a Harp?' Sat at the corner stool. Surveyed the scene. I was in no hurry. Just sit and let things unfold by themselves.

Pause.

It took a half an hour. Felt someone brush up against me. The back of my calf. I turned around. There she was. She had this amazing shock of blonde hair.

Pause.

She was beautiful.

LIV: I did think she was the prettiest one.

MARTIN: 'Hello.'
    'Hi.'
    'My name's Kurt.'
    'I've been...watching you.'
    'Really.'

Pause.

'Would you like to join my friends? We could...talk.'

Pause.

It was *working*.

Pause.

I went back to her table. Met her friends. They were all beautiful. We talked for a long time. They took turns telling me their stories. Then it was *my* turn. *A momentary sense of panic, of almost not going through with it.*

Pause.

But I did. I told them my story. I told them of my years in college. I told them of a friend I once had, his name was Martin, and how much I missed him. I told them of my bright future. How there was perhaps no limit to the things I could do. They sat enthralled. I had a completely captive audience.

Pause.

It was closing time before we knew it. I went to get my coat. I wasn't about to make the first move. I wanted to see if she would. *I knew she would.* And sure enough: 'Would you like to come back to my place? I don't live far from here. We could…talk some more.'
'That would be nice.'

LIV: 'Boy did I underestimate that one.'

MARTIN: And off we went. To her apartment. We sat on the floor. Silent. Then, she looked at me, took off her shirt. *She was lithe.* She leaned over, laid on my chest. She whispered: 'I want you.' *And I knew she meant it.* We stayed right there on the floor. Our clothes strewn about. 'I am yours. You own me. I am yours. You own me.' She kept saying that. Over and over. Whispering in my ear. The whole thing…it was…invigorating. To say the least.

Pause.

I stayed there for three days. When it was time for me to leave, she cried. 'Please, don't.' But I reassured her, told her I would see her again soon. I would return to her. This eased her mind somewhat.

Pause.

Of course, I never saw her again.

Pause.

IRIS: Oh God. Thinking back now. How it was then. Me, painting in that cramped living room. Working that canvas. I can only hope you understand. What it's like when everything in your life seems to be feeding that singular purpose.

Pause.

There were galleries that showed my work, such as it was. Small exhibits, tucked in a corner. Two small galleries in Soho and Tribeca. I would go – invariably Kurt had better things to do – and I would stand there. And wonder at how I came to be here. And how my life was in order, finally. Everything was in order.

KURT: Now, I am not going to complain, because basically I had everything that I wanted. I was working steadily. I had Iris. Things were going better than expected. I am not complaining.

Pause.

In many ways, my life was...calm. More calm and...sedate...than it had ever been.

Pause.

IRIS: It was seven months after we came to New York – We moved to a bigger apartment that Fall. In *Manhattan*. Already, he had published six stories. We'd go to parties. People would come up to him – and me – say how much they liked his work, that sort of thing, and he seemed quite humble about it. He deflected any praise with a wave and a quick comment.

KURT: Ah. It embarrasses me. People *gawking*.

IRIS: I was impressed by the way he was handling it all. It was happening quick for me, with my work, so I can't imagine what it must have been like for him. I'd pull him aside at the parties, or in the back of the cab, ask him what he was thinking. About his new life.

KURT: 'It's almost like it's not really happening to me. It's happening to someone else.'

IRIS: That's how he put it.

KURT: 'It's someone else's life.'

Pause.

IRIS: Then, the official book contract came.

KURT: A collection of my stories called *Isaac Greets the New Day* and *Collected Stories.*

IRIS: He didn't have to work a regular job. Not even part-time.

KURT: No more data entry for *me.*

IRIS: It wasn't a fortune, by any means. But…all he had to do was write. He could devote his whole life to it. Every waking hour, writing. Had to remind him to eat, or bathe, a lot of the time.

KURT: A lot on my mind.

IRIS: Shortly after that, after the contract, I lost my two days a week. No more going out. All seven days were for the writing. Pushed aside, again.

Pause.

LIV: And finally, I got a job. A *good* job. A better job than someone of my experience and background deserved. Assistant curator at the San Francisco Historical Society. Assistant to the assistant curator, actually. I hurried home, couldn't wait to share the news with him. I got home. Saw his coat and shoes by the front door. He must be home, in his room. I knocked on his door. 'Is it okay to come in?'

Pause.

No answer. I opened the door. He was sitting, looking out the window.

Pause.

'Hey. Guess who got a job today. Guess who is no longer 'just a waitress'?'

Pause.

'Martin'.

Pause.

I walked to his side. Looked at his face. My heart sank. I'd never seen that look on his face before.

Pause.

'Talk to me.'

Pause.

And then, weeks later, he finally did talk to me.

Pause.

KURT: The book was put together in four months. All the stories. Then the *fun* part began. From there it was this whirlwind. Of activity.

IRIS: He was gone all day. All night. Sometimes, he'd be out the door at eight in the morning, wouldn't come home 'til midnight, get up the next morning, do it all over again.

KURT: So many people to meet.

IRIS: Days would go by without me saying two words to him. Until the weekends. Then we would go out. To all the different homes of the people he had met. I was meeting all kinds of people. That I would not normally meet. They would ask about me, I told them I was a painter, and a few of them had even heard of me. He would disappear at these parties. Wouldn't see him for a while, but I didn't care. I was having fun.

KURT: Do you know what it's like? To have a whole room of people care who you are? Have a whole room of people want to know more about you? Hang on your every word? I bet you have no idea. I sure had no idea. Just how intoxicating it is.

Pause.

My editor would introduce me to these people. And they'd ask me about *Isaac.* What it was about. And I tell them. What I think the story's about. And they accept that as fact. Whereas, in truth, it is nothing more than conjecture. They ask me what I was thinking of when I wrote it, and I just…well, I just have to spout out some bullshit about what I think I was thinking about, because, obviously, you know, I don't know. You know? And again, they accept what I tell them as fact. 'That is what it is about. That's what he was thinking about.'

Pause.

Little do they know, right? What really goes on.

MARTIN: I was Kurt Mitchell. I was emboldened. I remember things as if I existed in a haze. A haze of lots

55

and lots and lots of sex. It was…sinful. My life carried on in that vein. Until one day, woke up knowing that I had to get out of that little hotel room. Just couldn't take it any more. The filthy bathroom, the ugly quite frightening men. So this meant that I had to get a job. Which, as it turned out, was very easy. Because in my mind, I was Kurt.

Pause.

And now…I could afford an actual *apartment.* At the top of Telegraph Hill. Whole new fantastic neighbourhood. Restaurants. Bars. A little postcard store halfway down the hill. An Italian bakery. A butcher shop. And a bookstore.

Pause.

The bookstore.

Pause.

I was there one day, university press section. Woman came up to me. Looking for a writer named Brooks, had I heard of him? No, I hadn't, but that didn't mean he didn't exist, let's go look. So we went on a hunt. For the writer named Brooks. Her name was Jennifer. Jennifer Something Polish. A graphic artist, something she enjoyed greatly. What did I do? I told her I was a writer. She asked me my name.
'My name is Kurt Mitchell.'
I should have seen this one coming.
'You mean this Kurt Mitchell?'
We were standing at the New Fiction table. *Oh fuck. Now what.*
'Yes. That is me.'
She looked it over.
'And this is you.'
She showed me his picture, inside flap.
'Umm…'

She looked at me for what seemed an eternity, shook her head, and simply walked away.

Pause.

I felt like shouting out: 'That should be me. I should *be* that Kurt Mitchell. By all rights.' But I said nothing. Just took the book, sat down, and read each and every story. Twice. As it turns out, they were pretty good. Slightly self-indulgent – and *derivative* – but… Some of the best work he has done.

Pause.

IRIS: One day, Kurt was out. His book was coming out in a few days, he was more than slightly out of sorts, I thought I'd try and pick up a nice surprise for him. Take his mind off things if I could. So I went to a neighbourhood I didn't usually visit. Kind of outta the way, but I was in the mood for an *adventure.*

Pause.

I saw him coming out of her apartment. Brownstone. His shirt was untucked, hair was tousled. She kissed him, full on the mouth. I had seen her before. Some party, I was sure. I watched her say goodbye to him. She grabbed at his crotch. He did not withdraw. He lingered a moment, then begged off.

KURT: I had had enough.

IRIS: He walked down the street, hailed a cab. And was gone.

KURT: Her name was Janelle. She was…an actress, I think. Something like that. Very talented. Very *limber.*

Pause.

IRIS: I stood on the sidewalk. For a long time. Until the sun had almost set. Then I left. Walked the whole way home. Thirty-eight blocks.

Pause.

That night, I didn't say anything to him. He had no idea he had been spotted.

Pause.

I packed up my supplies, canvas, charcoal, brushes, paints, put them down in the storage unit. Because the desire, the…whatever, was gone.

Pause.

People called me, the possibility of future shows, was I interested. But…I didn't call them back. And, so eventually, my phone stopped ringing altogether. And I remember, sometimes looking at him, thinking…thinking…

Pause.

Ah. Look at me. Two years later, I'm getting angry all over again.

MARTIN: So I left the bookstore. Tail between my legs. Was gonna go straight home. I walked up the street. Past the bar. Bigsby's. Hadn't been there in so long. Walked in, sat at the corner stool. 'Can I get a Harp?'

LIV: Started talking to him. See if I could get that aura again. 'Hi.'

MARTIN: 'Hi.'

Pause.

And yes, it started with that introduction.

Pause.

She was so beautiful. All that brunette hair. I wanted so badly to impress her. That I used the name that had become second nature to me. 'My name's Kurt.'

LIV: *Ah.*

Pause.

MARTIN: Thursday night came. And went. I couldn't see
her. Couldn't bring myself to go into that bar. Just sat in
my apartment.

Pause.

I thought about Liv. How she made me feel.

Pause.

I wasn't going to do it. No. Not anymore. No more lies.

Pause.

And I never used his name again.

Pause.

IRIS: It got worse once the book came out. Got some good
reviews. Not many people *bought* it…

KURT: …That's for damn sure…

IRIS: …But…he was making a name for himself. And with
that came new opportunities. All kinds of new women.
I knew what he was doing, and he knew I knew what he
was doing. But it didn't stop him. Just made him do it
more. Got so bad, I didn't know what I'd do.

Pause.

He was gone for weeks at a time. Then he just
reappeared. Without a word. Just wake up one morning,
and he'd be there, eating a bowl of cereal.

KURT: 'Hi. We're out of Cheerios.'

IRIS: And that would be that. Until his next little vacation.

Pause.

I asked him once, I finally worked up the courage:
'What do you think you're doing?'

KURT: 'With what.'

IRIS: *With what?* 'With me.'

KURT: 'Whatever.'

IRIS: 'But…what about me.'

KURT: 'You can do whatever you want, too.'

IRIS: 'What if I want to leave.'

KURT: 'Do what you want.'

Pause.

IRIS: I stayed around for another year. I don't know why.
Maybe I thought it was…punishment. Retribution. And
I deserved what I was getting.

Pause.

LIV: Four in the morning, I wake up alone, I see the light
on in his study. I walk to his door. I knock twice, then
I walk in. 'Martin, honey, it's late, come to bed.' He was
sitting in the middle of the floor. All the papers and
pages piled neatly in a corner, by the trashcan. His pens
on top of them.

MARTIN: 'I can't write anymore.'

LIV: 'What? Nonsense. Of course you can.'

MARTIN: 'Nope. It's all gone.'

LIV: 'Martin, listen to me. It's just a…what, it's a block.
It's temporary.'

Pause.

At this point, he produced the *New York Times.* Book
Review Section.

MARTIN: 'Look.'

LIV: He handed it to me. A review for a new novel called *The Splits*. 'Oh, look, this is your friend.'

MARTIN: 'He's gone and written a novel now. Supposed to be great.'

LIV: 'Good. Good for him.'

MARTIN: 'No. You don't understand.'

LIV: 'What.'

MARTIN: 'That should be me.'

Pause.

LIV: 'Martin?'

Pause.

MARTIN: 'Okay, no time like the present.'

LIV: And he told me. Everything. Iris. Kurt. His voice was shaking – I tried to hold his hand, but he wouldn't let me.

Pause.

And *then* he told me of one story in particular: *Isaac Greets the New Day*. Its…creation. Its history. It took him three hours. I listened to the whole thing. I wasn't so sure I believed it – It seemed so fantastic, so *bizarre*. But I listened. I was there for him.

Pause.

'But Martin, why didn't you *do* anything?'

Pause. MARTIN shrugs. Pause.

LIV: By the time he was done, the sun was up. He just looked out the window.

MARTIN: 'He stole from me. He's living my life.'

61

LIV: And then, he got up, walked out the front door.

Pause.

I should have went after him right then.

Pause.

KURT: Yes. We used to show each other what we wrote. Back in college. We'd walk for a while, talk about… whatever, women usually, Martin always wanted to talk about *women*, it was a thing for him, then we'd go across the street and play air hockey.

MARTIN: He was no better than me! By the end, I was probably even better than him!

KURT: *Hah.* Then we'd go have coffee and read each other's work. We did this twice, three times a week. So much writing going on. There was some crap in there, sure, but…

Pause.

But he was getting better. On the first read, you could tell how much better he was getting. I took it as a *challenge – Couldn't let that fucker be better than me, had to keep pace with him.* But there was no chance of that. He was getting too damn good. And every so often, he'd talk about sending something off, see what kind of response it would get. As soon as he had something he felt really had a chance.

Pause.

And then, one day, he called me at seven in the morning.

MARTIN: 'Meet me at the coffeeshop. As soon as you can.'

KURT: 'I have class at eight.'

MARTIN: 'I don't care. It can't wait.'

KURT: So I blew off class. And I went to meet him.
He looked like shit. Like he hadn't slept in days.

MARTIN: 'I have something to show you. You have to
read this. Now.'

KURT: And I read it. *Navy Pier*, it was called. All of eight
pages.

Pause.

It was good. Best thing he'd ever written. Maybe the
best thing I'd ever read. I didn't know what to say to
him. I mean…I…it was too good. Better than anything
I could ever *hope* to write. All I could tell him was:
'I think it's really good.'

MARTIN: (*Smiling.*) 'Yeah. It is, isn't it? I haven't shown it
to Iris yet. I wrote it for her. Think she'll like it?'

IRIS: *Yes.*

KURT: 'I'm sure she will.'

MARTIN: 'Hope so.

Pause.

The New Yorker is having a short story contest.
All submissions welcome.

Pause.

Maybe this is the one I send off. What do you think?'

KURT: 'I dunno.'

MARTIN: 'Yeah.'

Pause.

KURT: 'Can I keep it? This copy. Read it a few more
times.'

MARTIN: 'Sure. Wanted you to have it, anyhow.'

Pause.

KURT: And I took it back to my apartment. Read the thing five times. Each time finding something new. Poured over each word. Savoring it, cherishing it.

Pause.

That *fucker*. He had beaten me. I knew it.

Pause.

He called me later that night.

MARTIN: 'Ah. I don't think I'll send this one off. I think it needs more work. What do you think?'

KURT: 'Yeah. Maybe.'

MARTIN: 'Yeah.

Pause.

I almost showed it to Iris.'

KURT: 'Oh yeah?'

MARTIN: 'Yeah, but...no, not yet. I want it to be perfect.'

Pause.

KURT: I knew right then he wasn't going to do anything with it. And what a shame that would be. And then I thought about...all the possibilities. Other courses of action. So I took his story, changed the title – *Isaac Greets the New Day* – *Nathan* became *Isaac*, put my name on it, sent it out. It won the contest, they published it. The good folks at *The New Yorker*. And that was that. Nothing else to say, really.

Pause.

LIV: After that, after he finally told me everything, the whole story, he...disappeared. I had no idea what to do. After two days I went to the police. But...he hadn't been

gone long enough. 'Maybe he wants to be gone, Lady.'
So I called all the hotels in the book. At night, I walked
the streets. Trying to remember places he would visit.
But…he was nowhere.

Pause.

So I kept looking. For three weeks. I took some time off,
and I scoured the streets. Maybe he had left San
Francisco. If that was the case…well…I'd cross that
bridge when I got to it. But if he was in the city I would
find him. I knew that.

IRIS: I stayed for another year. Until we went to a book
signing. In Chicago, of all places. Only eight people
showed up. He was…damn near inconsolable. His
editor was there. 'This kind of thing is to be expected.'
But Kurt was having none of that. He took off after it
was over. Just got into a cab and drove away.

KURT: A city of how many million? And eight fucking
people show up? And this is to be expected?

IRIS: And I went back to our hotel room. And I waited for
him to come back. And I waited. The minutes passed.
Became hours. Of waiting. I walked out onto the
balcony. Looked at the stars. The sun came up. People
started appearing on the streets. Going to work. Leading
lives. It came to me, crystalline: 'He's waiting for me to
leave.'

KURT: *Exactly* what I was doing. Sat at the bar, in the
lobby, waiting to see her go.

IRIS: *All the mistakes, so many mistakes.*

Pause.

Packed my bags, and left. Went out on the street. Hailed
a cab. Checked into the Days Inn. Stayed there for ten
days, until I found a job and a place to live.

Pause.

And so when I first moved in, I walked around the old campus. So much had changed. In the two years.

Pause.

The coffeeshop is still there, of course. The arcade is gone, though. It's a bar now. I went in once. Just to look. And sure enough, the old air hockey table was in the back room. A couple was playing. From the looks of things, she was winning.

Pause. She smiles.

Hm.

Pause.

KURT: When I first came to New York, after I first sold the story, I got a call. The good people at The New Yorker wanted another one. For the next issue. Did I have anything they could use? Something that'd be ready in three days. 'Well, of *course.*' – *I was feeling cocky.* 'I could give you something tomorrow, if you'd like.' They said tomorrow would be ideal.

Pause.

And I had nothing. Not even an idea.

Pause.

I sat at my desk for five hours. And…nothing. Nary a word.

Pause.

Then I asked myself one question: 'What would Martin do?' And just like that the ideas, the words, they just… flowed through me. Five hours later, it was done. Fourteen pages. I went to their offices at ten. They read it right in front of me. They were quite pleased.

Pause.

How could I accept this? The knowledge that he's better than me. I couldn't. I fought it tooth and nail. For everything I wrote as Martin, I was sure to write one as myself, as Kurt. And I pushed myself. Extended myself farther than I had ever extended myself before. But, it did no good. Inevitably, what Martin wrote was better than what Kurt wrote. His were dazzling, mine were… *damn it*. Finally, just said fuck it. Stopped writing as myself. And no one would ever know.

Pause.

It's been like that ever since. Everything I have ever written, I have written as Martin.

Pause.

LIV: I had no idea I possessed the capacity to feel such loss. Martin was everywhere for me. I would smell his cologne on the bus; it was someone else. I would hear him, calling out to me; it was some random voice. I could feel myself sinking, vanishing. But I still kept looking. Driven, perhaps, by this sense of loss, this need to prevent myself from sinking.

Pause.

As it turned out, he found me. Down by the pier. He walked out of the wax museum, and right into me. Knocked me to the ground, spilling my purse. 'Hey. Why don't you fucking watch where you're going?' *Oh God it's him.* His beard was scraggly, his fingernails were long, he stank.

Nonetheless, in that first moment, there was real hope.

Pause.

'Oh, thank *God*. Martin.'

MARTIN: 'What? Where.'

LIV: 'What.'

MARTIN: 'Where's Martin? Been looking for him.'

LIV: 'What are you talking about?'

MARTIN: 'Martin. You see him? Is he here?'

Pause.

LIV: 'Kurt?'

MARTIN: 'Kurt? Who the hell is *Kurt.*'

Pause.

LIV: 'Please.'

MARTIN: 'And while we're at it, who the hell are you, anyway.'

LIV: '*Martin.* It's *me. Liv.*'

MARTIN: 'Liv. What an odd name. If I see Martin, I'll tell him you're looking for him.'

LIV: And then he walked away. I…could feel that sinking feeling return. Much stronger than before.

MARTIN: What the hell was I doing? I knew who she was; I knew who I was. Part of me wanted to just take her home, and forget this whole fucking thing. But… I didn't. I just didn't.

Pause.

Because I *did* like it out here on the streets. Something comforting and safe. Now, I know what you must be thinking. And I had no intention of living the rest of my life on the streets – I'm not *crazy* – It was just a good place to be at the time. And I had every intention of going back to Liv. But…a gut instinct. Telling me to stay out here.

Pause.

And that afternoon, down on the wharf, I saw an announcement. Taped to a bookstore window. Next to the announcement was a picture. It was my old friend, Kurt Mitchell. He was coming for a book signing. The very next day.

Pause. He smiles.

Yes. He was.

KURT: Ah…the book signing in San Francisco. That was a good one. Eighteen people. Eighteen whole people. We were just about done when a man walked in. This… bum, it looked like. Could *smell* him coming down the aisle. My editor was gonna call security, he was trying to get him outta there, but…he had bought a copy of the book, so…

MARTIN: I walked in. He was unchanged. After two years. Exactly the same.

KURT: So I figured, what the hell? Sign this guy's book. He brings it up to me. I look at him.

MARTIN smiles.

KURT: A sensation. A flash. From years ago. Ah.

Pause.

'Hi. How are you.'

MARTIN: 'Fantastic.'

KURT: 'How should I sign it?'

MARTIN: 'To my good friend.'

KURT: 'Alright.'

MARTIN: 'You know, you're much shorter than I'd pictured. From your jacket photo.'

KURT: 'They can be misleading.'

MARTIN: 'I'll say.'

Pause.

'And your face is fatter. Didn't envision you being so short, with such a fat face.'

KURT: 'Well. Sorry to disappoint.'

MARTIN: 'No need to apologise. You can't help it.'

Pause.

'I used to write.'

KURT: 'Really.'

MARTIN: 'Oh, yes. Didn't have what it took, though, apparently.'

KURT: 'Ah. That's too bad.'

MARTIN: 'Yep.'

Pause.

'You know, I used to have a friend named Kurt.'

KURT: 'Did you.'

MARTIN: 'Yes. But it was a long time ago.'

KURT: 'Ah.'

Pause.

I signed his book. Handed it back to him. He turned and was about to go, but he turned back to me.

MARTIN: 'I just wanted to tell you that you're a very talented writer, Mr. Mitchell. I admire you. Very much.'

KURT: 'Uh…thank you. Very much.'

MARTIN: 'But *Isaac*…now *that* was a story. The best thing you've written. By far.'

KURT: 'Well. Have a nice day.' And then he left.

MARTIN: I had nothing else to say.

Pause.

So I went home to Liv. I mean…*Olivia*.

Pause.

LIV: That night, after the wax museum, I went home. And…I have to tell you: I almost packed my things and left. Because no one should have to… But I found myself thinking back, focusing on one moment. Four nights after I moved in. Couldn't sleep. So frightened, wondering if I had fucked up horribly. And without saying a word, he turned to me, held me. I thought he was asleep. He kissed me, my neck, my shoulders, my stomach. He didn't even try to sleep with me. And at that moment, I was his. I knew he would have my heart forever. *And I had almost forgotten that.*

MARTIN: When I came home, Liv was gone. Her toothbrush, her toiletries, some of her clothes.

Pause.

It's been five days now.

Pause.

I've been so stupid. Selfish. I fucked up again.

KURT: The whole flight home from San Francisco, I found myself thinking about Martin. Standing there in the bookstore. Couldn't stop thinking about him.

LIV: And so the next morning, I decided to come here. New York. Take matters into my own hands.

Pause.

I make sure to call the San Francisco police as often as I can. But they never have any news.

Pause.

Left a message with Iris this morning. Took a few hours, but I found her. Felt she should know everything. Embarrassing as hell, calling your boyfriend's ex. But... what are you gonna do.

IRIS: I teach now. Art. I like it. More than I thought I would.

Pause.

One of the teachers asked me out the other day. How do you like *them* apples. He's very nice. He's very...there's potential there, maybe.

Pause.

He asked me what my story was. How I came to be here, teaching. I said, maybe another time, if I get to know you better.

Pause.

I'm painting again. Which is the really good news of all this. Just went out one day and bought brand new supplies. Feels good. Painting, painting, painting.

Pause.

Of course, I don't really have any furniture. The easel really is the cornerstone of the apartment. But...that's fine. I have no regrets. I am no victim.

Pause.

I don't know what else there is to say. I see Kurt's name in the paper. *The Splits* is doing pretty well, so...he's making the rounds. And I guess I'm happy for him. For the book, anyway. Because there's no point in holding grudges. Really. Grudge holding is quite counterproductive. That's what I always thought.

Pause.

But then, I came home tonight, a message on my answering machine. An actual message, who could it be. I ran to the machine, hit the play button.

LIV: 'Hi, uh…Iris. Uh…my name's Liv, and…ah…

Pause.

Yeah.

Pause.

I'm a…friend…of Martin's…I don't know if you remember…ah…and there's something you might not…so there's this story…*Isaac Greets the New Day*…that Kurt wrote. Martin wrote. And I'd…if you could call me back, the Hotel Edison, two one two – two nine six – five four zero zero – room five one two. I'd…appreciate it. Thank you. And ah…thanks.'

Pause.

IRIS: I go into my closet, dig out the story, that old black binder, and I read it. Three times. *And I see Martin in it. And I feel stupid for not seeing him all along.* And sure enough…there's that anger, primitive and resurgent.

Pause.

But I can't deal with it right now. I'll deal with it in the morning. So I walk to my easel in the corner, pick up my palette and my brush, and I stare at the canvas. New. Clean. Pure.

Pause.

And I don't think about anything. I just let the brush go where it goes.

LIV: I had appointments today with the New Yorker and with Viking Press. But...neither one seemed particularly interested in what I had to say. Got the ol' run-around.

Pause.

There's only one thing left to do now. Just hope it works.

KURT: I'm sitting in a bar here in New York. I'm all alone with a beer in front of me. And a feeling of...

Pause.

I still can't stop thinking about Martin. For *days* now. And I suppose about Iris. And about admitting things.

MARTIN: I've fucked up and I don't deserve her. Or she doesn't deserve me. Same thing.

Pause.

And she's never coming back.

Pause.

So I throw on my coat, and I'm out the door, because I can't stay here.

KURT: So I order another beer, take out my notebook, start writing the letter. Explaining everything. Send it to my editor in the morning. He'll know what to do with it. And...for the first time, the words flow out of me. Me. There is a spilling out. The words are coming out so fast, I'm worried I'll lose some. But I manage somehow. I get the whole story down. Exactly as it happened.

MARTIN: And now I'm on the streets again. Fog everywhere. Strangers' faces. No one that I know. No one that knows me. I walk past the transient hotel, past the front door, and there's that pang, that ache in my bones. I feel the pull of it.
But my name is Martin, I once had a friend named Kurt.

And now I'm in front of the wax museum. *Shame and regret.*
And now I'm in front of Bigsby's. *If I could do it all over again…*
There's a woman inside who looks like Liv. Of course it can't be, because it was a long time ago, and now she's gone, and I don't know how to find her, and I've fucked up again. *My name is not Kurt. It's Martin. Although it's very tempting.*

KURT: I finish the letter in six minutes. Martin will finally get the credit he deserves, and I'll get…control. I hope. I put down my pen and smile.

Pause.

That's when this woman comes up to me. *Oh God, why did she have to…*
'Hello, excuse me, but…aren't you Kurt Mitchell?'
She's beautiful. This beautiful brunette.
'Why yes. I am.'
'I'm sorry. Don't mean to disturb you. Just that…
I think you're very talented.'
That letter will never be sent.
'Well, thank you. Very much.'

Pause.

'Do you mind if I sit?'
'Please do.'
I buy her a drink.
'What's your name.'

LIV: 'Does it matter?'

KURT: (*Smiling.*) 'Suppose not.'

Pause.

She asks me my story, how I got my lucky break, and I give her the version most people know. And she's listening so intently. It's been so long since I had such a captive female audience – I'd forgotten just how good it feels.

LIV: 'I'd love to know more. And actually, there's a friend of mine who knows you.'

KURT: 'Really. Who.'

LIV: 'Why don't I get us some drinks first. Then we'll talk all about it.'

KURT: 'Sounds great.'

MARTIN: And now here I am on the pier. I've been here before. And I once wrote a story called *Navy Pier*. Behind me, few hundred yards away, there is a bookstore. Inside it, one of the shelves, is a story called *Isaac Greets the New Day*. You should read it sometime. Because were I a stronger man…if I could have only once…

Pause.

But my name is Martin. Martin. And this is who I am.

And this is where I am. All alone. Again. I look off, into the water. Murky and hopefully quite deep.

Pause. He smiles.

There's no place else to go.

KURT: I see her, waiting at the bar. She smiles at me.

She really is beautiful.

But there's something about her, something in her eyes. I'm just not sure. Not that it really matters, in the long run, what's on her mind.

LIV: *Please. Let me be strong. Please. Let me do this. Let me make it right.* That's all I want. To get things straightened out, and go back home to Martin. *Please.*

KURT: It doesn't really matter. Because whatever happens, I'll be okay. I'm always okay. Things just…bounce right off me. I don't know why. But I always emerge unscathed. Huh.

Pause.

LIV: *Please. Let me be strong.* 'Here you go.'

KURT: 'Thank you.'

LIV: 'You're welcome.'

KURT: 'So'.

LIV: 'So'.

KURT: 'Tell me about this friend of yours.'

Pause. LIV smiles.

MARTIN: I take one step forward. For an instant, I am hurtling down, between land and water. I see Liv. Her face. She is smiling. Then the waves take me in. *I'm sorry.*

The End.